NATIONAL GEOGRAPHIC

Common Core Readers

Ladders

CONNECTIONS to Nature

John Muir

John Muir was a **naturalist,** explorer, and writer who helped lead the early conservation movement in America. Muir spent much of his life working to save the American wilderness. He especially loved the Sierra Nevada mountain **range** of California. Muir spent a summer as a sheepherder in the Sierra Nevada.

Rambles

by Jennifer Boudart

Muir was an outdoorsman. He had previously completed a 1,609 kilometer (1,000 mile) walk from Indiana to the Gulf of Mexico. In 1868, Muir came to California looking for "any place that is wild." Now he set off on foot for Yosemite Valley. He brought a blanket, tea and bread, a plant press, and a notebook with him. Muir was in awe of the valley and the Sierra Nevada mountains, which he called the "Range of Light."

Muir stayed in California. He dreamed of exploring the Sierras, but he didn't have enough money. In the summer of 1869, a rancher named Mr. Delaney gave Muir a job. That job changed his life.

Muir and a group of men, dogs, and sheep made their way to high summer pastures above Yosemite Valley. Muir had never herded sheep before. But he had only to make sure the shepherd did his job. Beyond that, Muir would be free to explore the mountains. And these pastures were exactly where Muir wished to go! So on June 3, the group set out.

Muir climbed with the flock toward higher **elevations**. The beauty of Yosemite began to reveal itself. Muir explored canyons and caves. On June 8, the group set up camp along the Merced River. They stayed there for a month. Muir's duties were washing dishes, making bread, and finding lost sheep. He got some help from a local hunter's dog. As a naturalist, Muir studied wildlife, collected plants, and took notes in his journal.

Muir sometimes came across other people. He met local Indians, ranchers, loggers, miners, and some tourists. Yosemite was beautiful, and Muir wanted it to stay that way. He worried about the damage people might do to the mountain's **ecosystem**.

"Glorious days I'll have sketching, pressing plants, studying the wonderful **topography** . . ."

This is a sketch Muir drew of a canyon near Yosemite Valley.

The Merced River runs through Yosemite Valley.

Yosemite Falls

In early July, the group headed for higher elevation. They followed the Yosemite Trail. The sheep ate and climbed at their own pace. Muir did not like sheep. He called them "woolly bundles" and "busy nibblers." They were always getting stuck in bushes or running away. But thanks to the sheep, Muir was able to take daily "rambles" on his beloved mountain range. Muir was more curious than cautious. Once he tiptoed along a narrow ledge to the edge of Yosemite Falls. Another time, he climbed to the top of Mount Hoffman—about 3,352 meters (11,000 feet).

Mount Hoffman

One afternoon, Muir had a vision of his college professor staying at a hotel in the valley below him. His professor mentioned he might take a trip. But Muir didn't know for sure. Muir scrambled down the mountain just in case. After asking people in the hotel, Muir found his professor on a local trail. They spent the day visiting!

"Ramble to the summit . . . . the highest point in life's journey my feet have yet touched."

Muir's sketch of Half Dome

Cathedral Peak

In early August, bears killed a number of sheep. So the group kept moving. They made their last camp at about 2,743 meters (9,000 feet) in the Tuolumne Meadows. Muir explored the woods, meadows, and waterfalls. He climbed mountains. Muir became convinced that ancient **glaciers** had carved out Yosemite Valley. His theory was different from the claim that earthquakes had shaped the valley.

In early September, the group broke camp. They did not want to get caught in a snowstorm. They spent two weeks hiking back on the same path. The weather was cooling and the rivers were dropping. Summer was over. At trail's end, they counted the sheep. Three had been sold. Thirteen had been lost to predators or injury. Nine had been eaten in the camp. Muir had faced bears, starvation, and worse. And he had loved every minute of it! Muir's last journal entry told of his hope to experience the High Sierra again.

"I have crossed the Range of Light."

Muir's sketch of himself on one of his "rambles"

Muir described Tuolumne Meadows as a "flowery carpeted mountain hall."

Muir made this sketch showing how retreating glaciers chiseled away at the granite features of Yosemite Valley.

"Unless reserved or protected the whole region will soon or late be devastated ..."

Theodore Roosevelt (left) admired Muir and sought him out as a guide to Yosemite Valley.

Muir did see more of the Sierra Nevada. He went to work at a sawmill on Yosemite Creek. Muir lived in a cabin he'd built nearby. He spent his free time looking for evidence that glaciers had formed Yosemite Valley. Muir found an active glacier high in the mountains. An active glacier is one that retreats and advances. He published an article about it. He soon became known as an expert on Yosemite. In 1871, Muir moved away. But he wrote articles about threats to the region. He also fought to protect other wilderness areas in the country.

In 1889, Muir wrote articles about the damage sheep were causing to Yosemite's ecosystem. He asked Congress to save Yosemite by making it a national park. Parts of Yosemite became a national park in 1890. But Yosemite Valley and a grove of giant sequoia trees were not included. President Theodore Roosevelt took a trip to Yosemite with Muir in 1903. The naturalist persuaded Roosevelt to add these areas to the park. Muir helped form other national parks. He also formed a group called the Sierra Club. It still operates today. Muir wrote many more articles and books. He fought to protect natural land until he died at age 76.

Photo of Yosemite Falls in Yosemite Valley, 21st Century

Check In How did John Muir's exploration in California impact the rest of his life?

Wiffle® Chicken's Hike

by Mike McDonald

July 1–4 Mount Whitney, California

My name is Mike. I am a long-distance hiker. Out on the trail, I'm known as *Wiffle Chicken*. Many long-distance hikers have trail names. The first part of mine comes from my love of baseball. I played baseball on a college team. I love baseball so much, I brought a Wiffle ball and bat on the hike. And the chicken part? That was just for fun.

From July 1 to July 15, 2010, I hiked along the John Muir Trail in California. This trail is named after the great **naturalist,** John Muir. My journey was part of a longer hike along the Pacific Crest Trail. By the time I reached the John Muir Trail, I had been hiking for 44 days. I had already worn through two pairs of shoes!

Mount Whitney is 4,421 meters (14,505 feet) above sea level.

END
July 14–15
Yosemite Valley

July 11–13
Reds Meadow

July 8–10
Muir Pass

July 5–7
Rae Lakes

July 1–4
Mt. Whitney
START

Mono Lake

Lee Vining

Grant Lake

Mammoth Lakes

Lake Crowley

Toms Place

NEVADA
CALIFORNIA

■ John Muir Trail
■ Pacific Crest Trail
— Highway

N
W   E
S

Merced

South Fork San Joaquin

Lake Edison

Florence Lake

Owens

Bishop

Courtright Reservoir

Cedar Grove

Independence

Kern

0   5   10 Miles
0   5   10 Kilometers

On July 1, I awoke early to start my hike. The John Muir Trail runs 339.5 kilometers (211 miles). It begins at the summit, or top, of Mount Whitney. It runs through the Sierra Nevada mountain **range.** I soon faced an icy creek that I would have to **ford,** or cross. After fording the creek, my toes were numb. I still had many more hours of climbing.

At the rocky summit of Mount Whitney, I stood on the massive **granite** rocks. I looked out at the other mountain peaks. Soon other hikers joined me. We celebrated by playing a quick game of Wiffle ball.

July 5–7 Rae Lakes

On July 5, I reached the Rae Lakes with my friend, Breezy. We saw green, grassy meadows and a few pine and fir trees. The view was stunning. Snowy, granite peaks rose high above the sparkling, blue lakes.

Breezy and I forded the wide creek. We stood with sopping wet shoes on the other side. A hiker named Cheeseburger

If you were to hike around the Rae Lakes, you would travel 74 meters (46 miles).

didn't want his shoes to get wet. He decided to throw them across the creek. His first shoe landed with a thud on the creek bank. But he didn't have great aim with his second shoe. He threw it smack dab into the middle of the creek. Breezy sprinted down the trail and jumped into the creek. He managed to grab the shoe. Cheeseburger grinned. He almost had to hike with just one shoe.

What else was in my pack?

When hiking, every ounce in a pack adds up. It can start to feel like you are carrying an elephant on your back after a few miles of hiking. When I started the John Muir Trail, this is what was in my pack:

tent
sleeping pad
sleeping bag
first aid kit
hiking clothes
sleeping clothes
rain gear
bear canister
shoe micro spikes
ice axe
water filter
food
water bottles
maps
compass
pen
journal pages
toiletry items
Wiffle ball & bat
flip flops

My backpack and gear alone weighed

18 pounds

+ **34** pounds of food

52 pounds

To help with the weight, I carried only a few pages of my map book and a paperback book of short stories to read when I rested. But it was just half of the book. My friend, Swiss Miss, carried the other half.

July 8–10 Muir Pass

On July 8, we headed toward Muir Pass. We had one more night sleeping under the cover of a few pine trees. But soon we had climbed to an **elevation** of about 3,048 meters (over 10,000 feet) and there were no more trees. The snow covered everything except the granite rocks. The rocks had such a steep angle that the snow didn't stick. The sound of trickling water told us that snow was melting.

The higher we climbed, the more snow fell. The trail was covered. But now the snow wasn't melting. We struggled to find the trail to Muir Pass. We used our map and compass to guide us. We recognized Helen Lake and knew we were close. Soon we reached a stone hut at the top of Muir Pass. It was a great spot to look out over the blue lakes and snowy field below.

But I was soon distracted from the scenery. I noticed that my shoe had a small tear in the mesh. I kept hiking. Soon the mesh got caught on a branch. The small rip turned into a huge hole. I used duct tape and safety pins. I even sewed stitches with a needle and dental floss. After my shoe was fixed, I was ready to keep going.

This stone hut, known as Muir Hut, is a welcome shelter for hikers.

17

July 11–13 Reds Meadow

An alpine lake near
Reds Meadow

From Muir Pass we hiked down into
an area just over 2,133 meters (7,000 feet)
above sea level. There were many fir trees,
but the snow was gone. It was nice to walk
on dirt instead of rocks and snow. It was
July 11, and it felt as if we walked out of
one season and into another.

Reds Meadow was filled with wildlife.
As a novice naturalist, I loved observing
wildlife. That day I heard, "Eek! eek! eek!"
I stopped and waited. "Eek! eek! eek!"

A mouse sped across the trail. Behind the mouse raced a weasel-like creature. This was a pine marten. It quickly pounced on the mouse. The mouse dangled from the pine marten's mouth. The pine marten looked up at me. It seemed as if it was showing off! Then it ran down the trail and disappeared.

Shortly after that I saw bear footprints in the dirt and scratch marks on a rotting log. The scratch marks were a sign that a hungry bear had been digging for insects. I was careful to store my food properly so the bears would not try to get into it.

A Belly Full

Hikers need to eat nutritious foods that are rich in calories to supply their bodies with enough energy to exercise all day long. When the weather is colder, hikers need even more calories to keep warm. I estimated that I ate around 6,000 calories a day. This is 3 times the recommended daily allowance of 2,000 calories. Think of it like this:

If that was all I ate, I would have eaten at least 15 sandwiches and 20 apples every day to get enough calories!

about 6,500 calories
Now that's a big lunch!

July 14–15 Yosemite Valley

The John Muir Trail continued to drop. We were just one day away from Yosemite Valley, the end of the trail. The clouds were increasing, and the sky was getting darker. I heard thunder and saw lightning in the sky. An electrical storm had just passed us by. I walked the last few miles into Tuolumne Meadows. The green meadows rolled right into the awesome mountains.

A day later, on July 15, my friend and I hiked the final part of the John Muir Trail. We hiked past two powerful waterfalls as the Merced River fell into Yosemite Valley. Then we had a pizza and milk shakes, and rested our tired feet. My hiking friends and I had walked for 15 days, covering

339.5 kilometers (211 miles). We began at 4,417 meters (14,494 feet) above sea level and ended in Muir's beloved valley, at 1,219 meters (4,000 feet) above sea level.

The next day, I continued my journey on the Pacific Crest Trail. I saw more wildlife, including 14 bears and a few mice. I had worn through seven pairs of shoes and hiked for 4,264 kilometers (2,650 miles). But on October 9, I completed the trail and crossed the Canadian border. My hike had touched the borders of Mexico, the United States, and Canada. I had crossed the states of California, Oregon, and Washington.

I now live in Oakland, California. I'm not too far from where John Muir settled after his summer exploring the Sierras. I have maps spread out all over my kitchen table. I'm dreaming about where my next long hike will take me.

The upper waterfall of Yosemite Falls

Check In What parts of Mike McDonald's hike seemed to be the hardest?

IN THE ZONES

by Jennifer Boudart

A Guide to Yosemite National Park

Welcome to Yosemite, one of America's oldest national parks. Yosemite spans about 1,900 kilometers (1,200 square miles). Rising above are massive rock formations and mountain peaks. Below are green valleys and rushing rivers. And don't miss the waterfalls and glaciers. In fact, glaciers helped shape Yosemite. Slow-moving ice carved out the valley and its rock walls. The **elevation** in Yosemite ranges from about 550 meters to 3,962 meters (1,800—13,000 feet) above sea level. Yosemite includes part of the Sierra Nevada mountain **range.** As elevation changes, the landscape changes. The plants and animals change, too. Yosemite has hundreds of animal **species** and more than a thousand plant species. These plants and animals live in five zones. Each habitat is within zone. A field guide will help a hiker or a **naturalist** identify plants and animals.

ALPINE ZONE
2,896 meters and above (9,500 feet and above)

SUBALPINE ZONE
2,438–2,896 meters (8,000–9,500 feet)

UPPER MONTANE ZONE
1,829–2,438 meters (6,000–8,000 feet)

LOWER MONTANE ZONE
914–1,829 meters (3,000–6,000 feet)

FOOTHILL WOODLAND ZONE
549–914 meters (1,800–3,000 feet)

Visitors can access all five habitat zones in Yosemite.

482 Nearly 482 km (300 mi) of roads

1,287 about 1,287 km (800 mi) of hiking trails

Trails lead the way to waterfalls tucked into the foothills around Hetch Hetchy.

▼ The grey fox lives and hunts alone. It often takes refuge in thick chaparral.

▲ Whiteleaf manzanita is a chaparral shrub. Its thick, waxy leaves and red bark make it easy to identify.

▲ The blue oak does in fact have bluish-green leaves. Its acorns were once a favorite food of Native Americans living in the area.

▶ The mule deer is a common mammal in Yosemite, and it is the only species of deer found in the park.

FOOTHILL WOODLAND ZONE

Most visitors enter Yosemite from the west. This part of the park is at a low elevation. Very little snow falls here in winter, and summers are hot and dry. Visitors drive through the foothill woodland zone on their way to Yosemite Valley.

Most trees in this zone are species of oak. Shrubs also grow along the rocky hillsides. They form patches called chaparral. Foothill woodlands are in the northwest corner of the park. People hiking in this zone often see black bears and mule deer.

▲ Most black bears living in Yosemite are more brown than black. Hikers are safe watching these bears from a distance but should never try to feed them.

Mariposa Grove is located at an elevation of nearly 6,000 feet.

▲ Several unique sequoias grow in Mariposa Grove. One sequoia, the Grizzly Giant, is thought to be almost 2,000 years old.

▼ The Douglas fir has needles, but it is not a true fir tree. Its cones do not match the cones of true fir trees.

The solitary bobcat defends its territory most actively at dawn and dusk.

LOWER MONTANE ZONE

Above the foothills, visitors enter the lower **montane** zone. *Montane* means "of the mountains." Visitors can see nearby ridges and canyons. The montane zone is at a higher elevation. So winter often brings many feet of snow. The lower montane zone has the biggest variety of plant life. Its forests have deciduous trees, which shed their leaves, and **conifer** trees, which grow leaves year round. There are grassy meadows and some chaparral, too. Yosemite's biggest, oldest trees grow here. These conifers are called giant sequoias.

▶ The Sierra mountain kingsnake is not venomous and won't hurt people. However, it does eat rattlesnakes and is immune to their venom.

▼ Hikers may hear rather than see the elusive spotted owl. Its four-note call sounds like "hup, hoo-hoo, hooo."

▲ The Jeffrey pine's bark has a vanilla-like scent! It grows in exposed areas.

▼ The Sierra fence lizard is Yosemite's most visible reptile. Its behavior includes doing "push ups" to impress other lizards!

▼ The red fir's cones measure nine inches long. Cones don't drop off but instead disintegrate to release seeds.

▲ Lodgepole pinecones actually need fire to reproduce. Fire melts the cones' sticky coating, causing them to open and release seeds.

▶ Ostrander Lake is in the upper montane zone. Portions of surrounding lodgepole pine forest are fairly young because they're recovering from fires in 1987 and 1994.

UPPER MONTANE ZONE

The upper montane zone begins at 1,829 meters (6,000 feet). The winters are cold and snowy. Many conifers grow here. Conifers have needle-shaped leaves. The leaves drop and are replaced a few at a time. Many people call these trees "evergreens." Most trees in the upper montane zone are species of fir, pine, hemlock, and juniper. There are some wet bogs and flowering meadows here, too. Ground squirrels and blue grouse live on the forest floor. Porcupines and gray owls live in the treetops.

▶ The golden-mantled ground squirrel resembles a chipmunk. It has a yellow-brown patch, or "mantle," on its neck and shoulders.

29

SUBALPINE ZONE

The subalpine zone has long, cold, and snowy winters. There are trees and grassy meadows in this zone. This is the highest elevation at which trees can grow. Trees often grow at odd angles. This helps them survive strong winds. Mountain lions and Sierra Nevada bighorn sheep roam in this zone.

Tuolumne Meadows perches at 2,621 meters (8,600 feet). Only one road provides access, and for almost half of the year, the area is closed because of snow.

◀ The alpine chipmunk is active by day, foraging for seeds and fungi. It stores away its food for winter.

▼ Sierra Nevada bighorn sheep are an endangered species. Consequently, hikers rarely see them.

Life is harsh but beautiful in the alpine zone. Shrubs grow between boulders. Wildflowers and alpine butterflies thrive in summer. Many alpine areas can only be reached by hiking in places where there are no roads or trails.

ALPINE ZONE

◀ The Sierra skipper is one of approximately 60 butterfly species found above 3,048 meters (10,000 feet). Females deposit their eggs on alpine grasses.

▼ Hikers may spot yellow-bellied marmots sunbathing on rocks. These large rodents form colonies.

Many species of monkeyflowers flourish at various elevations in Yosemite. This mountain monkeyflower dots alpine meadows.

Check In How does the zone at the lowest elevation differ from the zone at the highest elevation?

Discuss | Information from the Past and Present

1. Why do you think the three pieces in this book relate to the theme of *Connections to Nature*?

2. The first two pieces take place in the same area. How are the two accounts alike and different?

3. In the first account, John Muir takes a short trip into the Sierra Nevada. How does his first trip affect the plans he makes after that?

4. What did you find most interesting about Wiffle Chicken's hike?

5. Think about the information you read about the Sierra Nevada mountain range and Yosemite National Park. Describe the geography of the area. How does the geography impact the plant and animal life?

6. What do you still wonder about Yosemite National Park? What would you like to learn more about?